CW01432142

3303292977

At last, a biography of the crucial member of the Oxford research team that gave the world penicillin. Norman Heatley's technical ingenuity ensured its success. No one merits higher praise for getting the greatest advance in 20th century medicine under way, but remarkable modesty kept him from deserved acclaim for far too long. Congratulations to David Cranston and Eric Sidebottom on this admirable account of his life and achievements.

Professor Max Blythe, Green Templeton College

I feel privileged to write an introduction to this biography of Norman Heatley whom I knew as a friend and parishioner for many years. He was the most human and humble person you could ever imagine, and his work on the development of penicillin will last for ever.

Paul N. Rimmer, Vicar of Marston, 1959-90

It is remarkable that while his colleagues were receiving the world's acclaim for the development of penicillin, the crucial contribution of Norman Heatley was largely forgotten. What is equally remarkable is that, in subsequent years, he never expressed even a hint of disappointment or envy at his exclusion. Norman's modesty was not regarded as a weakness by those who knew him but as a life-long feature of his personality which led to trust and friendship. It is a rare quality in the competitive arena in which many scientists spend their professional lives struggling for recognition.

Sir James Gowans, Fellow of the Royal Society

Penicillin
and the
Legacy of Norman Heatley

Penicillin

and the

Legacy of Norman Heatley

David Cranston and Eric Sidebottom
Illustrated by Valerie Petts

Norman Heatley working at the laboratory bench c. 1940

David Cranston completed his medical training in Bristol and worked in Exeter and Bath before coming to Oxford for post-graduate doctoral research. He is a Fellow of the Royal College of Surgeons of England and is currently Consultant Urological Surgeon in the Oxford University Hospitals NHS Trust, Associate Professor of Surgery in the Nuffield Department of Surgical Science and a Fellow of Green Templeton College, Oxford. Outside medicine he serves as a licensed lay minister in the Church of England and is on the board of the Oxford Centre for Mission Studies.

Eric Sidebottom spent his childhood in the Peak District of Derbyshire, his secondary education in Lancashire and his medical education in Oxford and London (Barts) where he qualified in 1963. He moved back to Oxford and completed a DPhil with Henry Harris and was then appointed to a University Lecturership in Experimental Pathology and as Nuffield Research fellow and Medical Tutor at Lincoln College. In the early 1990s he spent 5 years as Assistant Director of Clinical Research at The Imperial Cancer Research Fund (now CRUK). Since then he has been a freelance Education and Research consultant increasingly studying and writing about the History of Oxford Medicine and the role of Disease in World History.

Valerie Petts first started training as a lab technician in Professor Howard Florey's department in Oxford before working in clinical immunology research in London and Sydney and has now been painting full-time since about 1990. She has had numerous exhibitions in England and has also exhibited in Tokyo and Cape Town. She has illustrated five books including Oxford Words and Watercolours, Consider England *and a visitors' book for the National Trust.*

FOREWORD

This is the real (and surprising) story behind the greatest medical achievement of the twentieth century.

I am amazed that it has taken so long to tell the story of Norman Heatley, the scientist whose talents made the development of penicillin, the world's first antibiotic, possible. He was truly 'the right man in the right place at the right time'. He deserves to be remembered, and this book will help to ensure that the true story of the birth of antibiotics is not forgotten.

The authors are to be congratulated on giving us this sensitive and sympathetic record of the life of 'the unsung hero of penicillin', Norman Heatley.

Professor Matthew Freeman
Sir William Dunn School of Pathology.

ACKNOWLEDGEMENTS

Norman Heatley is one of the unsung heroes of the twentieth century, without whom penicillin may never have come into the armamentarium of the medical profession. Sir William Osler, Regius Professor of Medicine in Oxford at the beginning of the twentieth century wrote that:

> *Humanity has but three great enemies: fever, famine and war; of these by far the greatest, by far the most terrible, is fever.*

Norman Heatley's role in fighting this great enemy was monumental, the public recognition for his role in this, small and late in coming. We hope this short book will continue to keep alive his memory and his achievements.

Both of us knew him in different circumstances, one (ES) as a colleague at the Dunn School, the other (DC) as a fellow member of the congregation of St Nicholas Church in Old Marston. It has been a privilege and an education to research his life and present it in this book.

We are grateful to members of the Heatley Family especially Rose and Tamsin Heatley who have made helpful comments and corrections and provided a great deal of material for this book.

We also thank Professor Matthew Freeman for his foreword and to Rev Paul Rimmer, Professor Max Blythe and Sir James Gowans for their kind words of commendation.

Valerie Petts has enhanced the book tremendously by her beautiful watercolours, while Tony Gray has been very helpful and patient as both editor and publisher through his company WORDS BY DESIGN.

For our wives

Rosie Cranston and Margaret Sidebottom

and in memory of Nilay Patel,
Consultant Urological Surgeon Oxford 1975-2014.

CONTENTS

The Nobel Prize in Physiology or Medicine 1945

"for the discovery of penicillin and its curative effect in various infectious diseases"

Sir Alexander Fleming

Ernst Boris Chain

Sir Howard Walter Florey

CHAPTER 1: INTRODUCTION

Everyone has heard of penicillin. Most people have heard of Alexander Fleming and credit him with the discovery of penicillin. Some have heard of Howard Florey and Ernst Chain and the Nobel Prize they were awarded in 1945 with Fleming for their work on penicillin. Fewer people know the story of Norman Heatley and his role in the development of penicillin, largely unrecognised until he was awarded an honorary Oxford DM in 1990 (the second ever awarded, and the first time in Oxford's 800-year history that it was awarded to a non-medic).

Heatley's role was neatly expressed in a Florey centenary lecture given in 1998 by Sir Henry Harris (Florey's successor as Professor of Pathology at Oxford) who succinctly summed up the story of penicillin by saying:

> *Without Fleming, no Florey or Chain, without Chain no Florey, without Florey no Heatley, without Heatley no penicillin.*

It could also be added, 'Without Oxford no Fleming', as Fleming's lasting fame was due to the work done in Oxford demonstrating that penicillin was of clinical use. Looking back, it is not unreasonable to claim that the introduction of the world's first antibiotic was the most important medical advance of the twentieth century.

Although Norman Heatley is the least celebrated of the main characters in the penicillin 'cast', the legacy he has left behind is very important, not only for medicine but also for historians of science and medicine. He was a prolific diarist, and both his diaries and his lab notebooks are very detailed. This contrasts greatly with Ernst Chain who kept poor records and whose reliance on memory led him to make claims that could not later be substantiated. This profound difference towards records was an important part of the background which led Heatley to escape from Chain's supervision and seek to work under Florey's guidance. There is a page in Heatley's lab notebook for 1939 with just two simple entries:

Sept 3rd   *War declared by Great Britain against Germany*
Oct 1st   *Work began with Professor Florey*

These two events in Heatley's life seem to have had a similar momentous significance for him. Much later in his life, indeed after retirement, and at the urging of colleagues and friends, Norman set down four pages of notes on why he couldn't work under Chain.

Before considering Norman Heatley, the unsung hero of the penicillin story, it will be helpful to look at both the types of *Penicillium* mould and the history of penicillin. The look at 'types' offers a little scientific explanation. Contrary to popular belief, the history (considered in the next chapter) did not start in 1928 with Alexander Fleming but a long time before. Its story is often hidden, sometimes obscure, frequently convoluted and at times controversial.

The types of Penicillium
Penicillin is an antibiotic. Antibiotics are substances made by living cells, in contrast to chemotherapeutic agents, such as sulphonamides, that are synthesised chemicals. Penicillin originates from a type of fungus called *Penicillium*. The genus was first described in the scientific literature by Johann

Heinrich Friedrich Link in 1809. He described three species – *Penicillium candidum*, *Penicillium expansum* and *Penicillium glaucum* – all of which produce a brush-like conidiophore. Conidia are the non-motile spores of a fungus and the name is taken from the Greek word for dust, 'konis'. This in turn is what gave penicillin its name, for it is derived from the Latin root *Penicillium*, meaning a 'painter's brush', and refers to the chains of conidia that resemble the bristles of a broom.

Over 300 species of the genus *Penicillium* have now been identified. The genus includes a wide variety of species but the drug Penicillin is produced by *Penicillium chrysogenum* (previously known as *Penicillium notatum*). This is the type noted by Fleming in 1928 which he found to inhibit the growth of certain bacteria (although in his 1929 publication he called it *Penicillium rubrum*).

Other species have different functions. Some play a role in the production of cheese and of various meat products. *Penicillium camemberti* and *Penicillium roqueforti* are the moulds on Camembert, Brie, Roquefort, and many other cheeses. *Penicillium nalgiovense* is used to improve the taste of sausages and hams, and to prevent colonisation by other moulds and bacteria. *Penicillium bilaiae* is found in the soil and can enhance the uptake of phosphate by root structures while feeding off plant waste products and, as a result, stimulate plant growth.

Penicillium marneffei, by contrast, is a species endemic in South-east Asia, which presents a threat of systemic infection to AIDS patients. *Penicillium verrucosum* produces ochratoxin A, one of the most abundant food-contaminating toxins, while *Penicillium expansum* and *Penicillium funiculosum* are both plant parasites.

Therapeutic penicillins are used in the treatment or prevention of many different bacterial infections, usually caused by Gram-positive organisms. They are all β-lactam antibiotics; that is to say they are antibiotic molecules with a β-lactam nucleus.

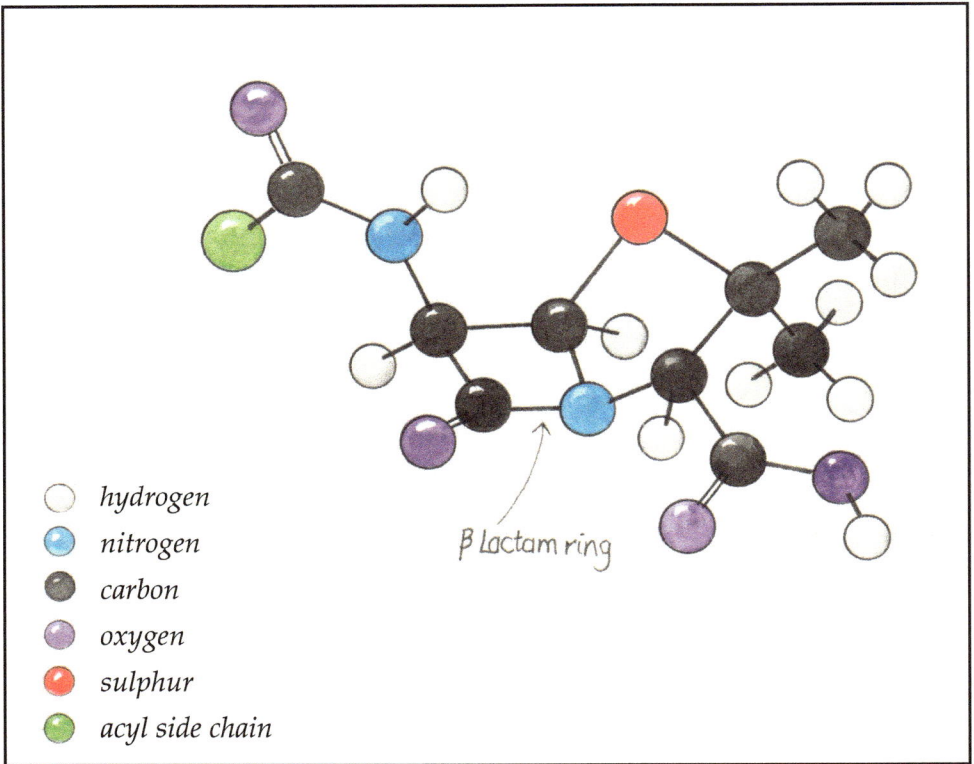

hydrogen
nitrogen
carbon
oxygen
sulphur
acyl side chain

β Lactam ring

Molecular structure of penicillin molecule

Penicillin kills susceptible bacteria by specifically inhibiting the enzyme that is responsible for catalysing (accelerating the reaction of) the final step in the construction of the cell wall. Thus it only works on growing, dividing bacteria and as such it is 'bacteriolytic' not 'bacteriostatic'. In other words, it kills rather than simply inhibits growth of bacteria. It should not be used together with other antibiotics, which are bacteriostatic, as they would be ineffective if the bacteria are not dividing. Penicillin is truly a 'magic bullet' since it acts on a chemical reaction that occurs in bacterial cells but not animal cells. The only harm it can cause to human patients is through allergic reactions.

Bacteria can build a resistance to penicillin by synthesizing *β-lactamase*, an enzyme that defends the bacterial walls by splitting the β-lactam ring. Combining the penicillins with β-lactamase inhibitors such as clavulanic acid (in the antibiotics amoxiclav or augmentin) can counteract this defence.

CHAPTER 2: THE HISTORY OF PENICILLIN

Several ancient cultures, including those in Greece and India, used moulds and other plants to treat infection. However, they were not able to distinguish or distil the active component in the moulds. Over the centuries there have been many old remedies where moulds have been used in this way.

Imhotep was an Egyptian polymath in the twenty-seventh century BC. An architect, engineer, high priest and physician, he was also possibly the author of a medical treatise which was remarkable in its day for being devoid of magical thinking – the so-called 'Edwin Smith Papyrus'. This ancient Egyptian medical text (named after the dealer who bought it in 1862) is the oldest known work on surgical trauma and may have been a manual for military surgery. There are other ancient papyri, for example the Ebers Papyrus and the London Medical Papyrus, but these are medical texts based on magic, whereas the Edwin Smith Papyrus presents a rational and scientific approach to medicine based on observation and experience, detailing 48 cases of injury, fractures and wounds. Each case describes the type of the injury, examination of the patient, diagnosis and prognosis, and treatment. Some surface infections were treated with mouldy bread!

In the second century BC, soldiers in the army of King Dutugemunu, King of Sri Lanka, were reported to have stored oil cakes (a traditional Sri Lankan sweetmeat) for long periods in their hearth lofts before embarking on their military campaigns. They made a poultice of the cakes with which to treat wounds. It is assumed that the oil cakes served the dual functions of desiccant and antibacterial agent. In Serbia and in Greece, mouldy bread was a traditional treatment for wounds and infections, while Russian peasants used warm soil as treatment for infected wounds.

In Poland in the seventeenth century wet bread was mixed with spiders' webs containing spores to treat wounds, a technique that was mentioned by Henry Sienkiewicz in his 1884 book, *With Fire and Sword*. In England, John Parkington, who was an apothecary and herbalist to King Charles I, advocated the use of mould in his 1640 book on pharmacology.

Sir John Scott Burdon Sanderson was born in 1828 and completed his medical education in Edinburgh and Paris before moving to London where he became Medical Officer for Health for Paddington in 1856. When diphtheria appeared in England in 1858, he was sent to investigate the disease at the different points of outbreak, and also carried out similar inquiries into the cattle plague and cholera. However, in 1871 he observed and reported that culture fluid covered with green mould (probably *Penicillium*) inhibited the growth of microenzymes (bacteria). Yet he seems to have taken this observation no further, even though he was prominent in the development of the germ theory of infectious disease. In 1882 he was appointed to the newly created Waynflete Chair of Physiology in Oxford and in 1895 succeeded Sir Henry Acland as Regius Professor of Medicine in Oxford, a post that he held until 1904. He died in 1905 and Sir William Osler succeeded him as Regius Professor.

Joseph Lister was born in 1827 and was present at the first surgical procedure carried out under anaesthetic in the United Kingdom in 1846. He became a Fellow of the Royal College of Surgeons in 1852 and in 1860 was appointed to the chair of Surgery in Glasgow. He had read Pasteur's work on micro-organisms and decided to experiment by exposing surgical wounds to dressings soaked in carbolic acid. He had also read that carbolic acid was a powerful antiseptic that killed cattle parasites and sterilised sewage in fields outside the city of Carlisle. His use of carbolic acid for hand washing, sterilizing instruments and spraying in the theatre while operating, dramatically lowered the infection rate and became the adopted technique in many countries.

He was prompted by Sanderson's discovery to investigate these antibacterial observations further, and in 1871 demonstrated that urine samples contaminated with mould prevented the growth of bacteria. He also described the antibacterial action of what he called *Penicillium glaucum* on human tissue. When a nurse at King's College Hospital had skin wounds that did not respond to any antiseptic, she was given another substance that cured her. Lister's registrar informed her that it was called *Penicillium*. There is no record that Lister took the penicillin experiments further, but for his other work he is known as the 'father of antiseptic surgery'.

He received many honours in his lifetime – Queen Victoria created him a Baronet in 1883 and further raised him to the peerage as Baron Lister of Lyme Regis in 1897. He was President of the Royal Society from 1895 to 1900, a rare honour for a surgeon. He was one of the original twelve members of the Order of Merit, and King Edward appointed him as a Privy Councillor in 1902. He is one of only two surgeons to have a public memorial in London (on Portland Place) and he even has a bacterial genus, Listeria, a slime mould genus, Listerella, and a Research Institute, The Lister Institute of Preventive Medicine, named after him.

In 1875 a distinguished English physicist named **John Tyndall** was researching bacteria and trying to find if there was a random dispersion of bacteria in the atmosphere. In order to do this, he set up open test tubes containing broth.

Tyndall prepared 100 tubes and placed them close to each other. He kept the tubes open to expose them to the air, or to his 'optically pure air', free from particles that he had ingeniously produced. The next day he noticed that the broth in some of the tubes remained clear, which proved that no bacteria had fallen into them, despite the fact that all the tubes were kept open. This indicated that Tyndall's theory about the even distribution of bacteria in the atmosphere was wrong. He also showed that some of the contaminated tubes did not contain living bacteria. He had discovered bacterial spores which could survive boiling. He introduced 'tyndallisation', intermittent steaming, which then killed the spores.

Tyndall also observed that on the surface of some of the tubes there was an "exquisitely beautiful" *Penicillium* mould. He believed that there was a battle between the bacteria and the mould and, "in every case where the mould was thick and coherent, the bacteria died or became dormant and fell to the bottom as a sediment." Tyndall only studied the physical properties of *Penicillium notatum*, observing that *Penicillium* was able to destroy bacteria falling into the tubes from the air, but he was unaware at that stage that bacteria could cause disease. He is said to have demonstrated these findings to the Royal Society in 1875.

Tyndall succeeded Faraday at The Royal Institution. He was an inspiring teacher and lecturer and is reputed to have said about teaching, "I do not know a higher, nobler or more blessed calling." Today's universities and schools might well note this.

Louis Pasteur was born on 27 December 1822, in Dole, France. Although trained as a chemist, he became famous as a microbiologist and is recognised as one of the founding fathers of microbiology. He helped to show that microbes were responsible for souring alcohol, for fermentation and for wound infections. He developed the process that bears his name, pasteurisation, whereby bacteria in fluids are destroyed by heating the fluids and then allowing them to cool. Further work in this area led his team to discover vaccinations for anthrax and rabies. However, he also observed that cultures of the anthrax bacilli, when contaminated with moulds, became inhibited. There is some evidence that he identified the strain as *Penicillium notatum*, although firm proof is lacking.

In 1894 a young student by the name of **Ernest Duchesne** entered the Military Health Service School of Lyons, France. One day three years later, he observed that the Arab stable boys at the army hospital kept their saddles in a dark and damp room in order to encourage mould to grow on them. When he asked them why, they told him that the mould helped to heal the saddle sores on the horses. Intrigued, the young medical student prepared a series of experiments in which he tested the effect of French tap water on mould and discovered that the mould was significantly diminished when exposed to the water.

After detailing 19 different experiments, he concluded that the presence of *Penicillium glaucum* inhibited bacterial growth. He also prepared a solution of the mould and injected it into a guinea pig, showing that an animal inoculated with a normally lethal dose of typhoid bacilli would be free of the disease if the animal were also inoculated with *Penicillium glaucum*. At the age of 23 he submitted a doctoral thesis entitled "Contribution to the study of vital competition in micro-organisms: antagonism between moulds and microbes." This was the first study to consider the therapeutic capabilities of moulds resulting from their antimicrobial activity.

As Duchesne was an unknown 23-year-old, the Institute Pasteur did not even acknowledge receipt of his dissertation. He urged for more research but unfortunately, after receiving his degree, his army service prevented him from developing his research. He did not claim that the mould contained any antibacterial substance, only that the mould somehow protected the animals. He even managed to cure infected guinea pigs from typhoid (although the type of penicillin isolated by Fleming does not do this).

At the time Duchesne carried out his observations, the term *Penicillium glaucum* was used as a catch-all phrase for different fungi, although not for *Penicillium notatum.* Unfortunately, the mould was not preserved, which makes it impossible to be certain today which fungus might have been responsible for the cure. Duchesne was honoured posthumously in 1949, four years after Fleming, Florey and Chain had received the Nobel Prize for their work.

Alexander Fleming was born in Ayrshire in 1881. At the age of 20 he inherited some money from an uncle and so was able to start at St Mary's Hospital Medical School in London where he qualified with distinction in 1906. Although he had planned to train as a surgeon, Fleming took the post as assistant bacteriologist to Sir Almroth Wright, a pioneer in vaccine therapy and immunology. This enabled him to remain at St Mary's and compete for the hospital's rifle team, of which he was a key member.

In 1908 Fleming gained a BSc degree with Gold Medal in Bacteriology, and became a lecturer at St Mary's where he remained until the start of the First World War in 1914 when he joined up and served as a captain in the Royal Army Medical Corps. He worked in a number of battlefield hospitals along the Western Front in France, where he witnessed the death of many due to sepsis. This became a stimulus for him to search for an anti-bacterial agent on his return to St Mary's Hospital in 1918, where in due course he was appointed Professor of Bacteriology.

During the 1920s his search first led him to lysozyme, an enzyme with an antibacterial effect that damages cell walls. Lysozyme is present in a number of bodily secretions including tears, saliva, human milk and mucus, as well as white blood cells. By 1927 Fleming was investigating the properties of staphylococci. Some of his colleagues regarded him as a brilliant researcher, but also one who had an untidy laboratory. Before leaving for a holiday with the family in August 1928, he had stacked all his cultures of staphylococci on a bench in a corner of his laboratory.

When he returned on 3rd September 1928 he noticed that one culture was contaminated with a blue-green fungal mould, and that the colonies of staphylococci immediately surrounding the fungus had been destroyed. Other staphylococci colonies farther away were normal and Fleming famously remarked, "That's funny." He concluded that the mould was releasing a substance that was inhibiting bacterial growth. He grew a pure culture of the mould, which he called *Penicillium rubrum* in his first publication (it turned out to be *Penicillium notatum*). After some months of calling the filtrate 'mould juice', he named it 'Penicillin' on 7 March 1929. This was a masterstroke since it was a catchy name that even though it was first used for the crude extracted mould juice, continued to be used by the Oxford team for the purified antibiotic. It has been said that if the Oxford team had coined a different word for the purified antibiotic, much of the acrimony between Oxford and St Mary's might have been avoided.

Fleming published his discovery in 1929, in the British *Journal of Experimental Pathology,* but little attention was paid to his article, or to the subsequent lecture he gave to describe his new discovery. However, it is interesting to note that Howard Florey was an editor of the journal at that time who should have known of Fleming's work. Fleming continued his investigations, but found that cultivating *Penicillium* was difficult, and that after having grown the mould it was even more challenging to isolate the antibiotic agent. He employed two young post-graduates to help in this task, Stuart Craddock and Frederick Ridley, but their work is barely mentioned in Fleming's paper.

Ronald Hare, who was working at St Mary's at the time of Fleming's discovery and subsequently became Professor of Bacteriology at Birmingham University, has made a careful study of Fleming's work and the conditions surrounding it. He feels that Fleming did not understand the experiments that Craddock and Ridley carried out in their attempts to isolate the active principle from the mould juice. He certainly didn't report them in his paper.

Fleming's impression was that because of the problem of producing it in quantity, and because its action appeared to be rather slow, penicillin would not be important in treating infection. Fleming also became convinced that penicillin would not last long enough in the human body (*in vivo*) to kill bacteria effectively, and although he continued with further research into the 1930s, he was unable to refine usable penicillin and so abandoned further research.

Cecil Payne was a young man training at St Mary's Hospital when Fleming discovered penicillin. He obtained a sample of the mould and took it with him when he moved to a junior lectureship at Sheffield in 1930. He grew the mould using Fleming's method, filtered the resulting mould juice, and applied it first to some patients with skin infections. No improvement was obtained but Payne then applied his filtrate to the eyes of four babies who were suffering from 'ophthalmia neonatorum', an infection normally caused by Neisseria gonorrhoea, the bacterium usually responsible for causing gonorrhoea (the 'clap'). In three cases he noted a marked improvement. He also successfully treated a miner with an infected penetrating wound in his eye.

Unfortunately Payne never published this work and never repeated the treatment with mould juice. He quickly moved on to another post with different interests. However, when Florey arrived in Sheffield in 1932 as Professor of Pathology, Payne reported his penicillin treatments to Florey who recorded this work in the two-volume book on antibiotics published in 1949. Subsequently two medical historians in Sheffield, Milton Wainwright and Harold Swan, read Florey's account, discovered that Cecil Payne was still alive, and interviewed him to confirm the story. They were able to find the patient records of two of the babies in the hospital archives. They wrote up a detailed account of these events in the journal *Medical History* in 1986.

During the next twelve years (1928-1940), Fleming grew and distributed the original mould, trying unsuccessfully to get help from any chemist who may have had enough skill to make a stable form of it for mass production. Harold Raistrick, together with colleagues Clutterbuck and Lovell, based at the London School of Hygiene and Tropical Medicine, tried in 1932 to extract the active principle from mould juice, but again found it unstable and difficult to work with. There was no further progress until Howard Florey (who now held the Chair of Pathology in Oxford) and Ernst Chain (a biochemist who was working with Florey) asked a young research chemist in their department to help them with their work on penicillin. His name was Norman Heatley.

CHAPTER 3: NORMAN HEATLEY – HIS EARLY LIFE

Norman George Heatley was born on 10th January 1911 in Woodbridge, Suffolk, a town on the river Deben which had been inhabited since the Neolithic period and had become a centre for boat building, rope-making and sail-making from the Middle Ages. Edward III and Sir Francis Drake both had warships built there.

Norman's father came from Cheshire where the family were yeoman farmers living in a large cottage near Knutsford. He knew little about his paternal grandparents, except that his grandfather was a litigious man who took part in several lawsuits, while his grandmother had lost her first husband and all her children in a smallpox epidemic. She then married Norman's grandfather, seemed to harbour no bitterness as a result of her previous sorrows, and became a devoted wife and mother to her husband and their four children.

Thomas George Heatley worked on the family farm until he was 21 when he entered the Royal 'Dick' Veterinary College in Edinburgh. He did well, winning the Fitzwygram prize in 1892 as the top student, and after graduation worked in the Hollesley Bay Colony in Suffolk. Opened in 1887, this was one of a number of institutions across Britain which housed a labour colony for the London unemployed with the aim of teaching them practical skills prior to emigration to Australia or New Zealand where they could then better their lot in life.

After qualifying, his father had the title of Professor of Veterinary Science and taught two classes a day. As he enjoyed riding, racing, sailing and shooting, he decided to teach one class before breakfast and the second after dinner, leaving the whole day free for outdoor pursuits! He remained there for two years although he realised that this was not a long-term option. He subsequently left to set up a veterinary practice in Woodbridge with a family home on the main street boasting a large rear garden.

In 1916 Norman's father joined the Royal Army Veterinary Corps and travelled to Le Havre where he worked in a large veterinary hospital, treating some of the many horses and mules that were used in the First World War. When he developed Bright's disease (inflammation of the kidneys accompanied by high blood pressure and oedema), he became so ill that the army began discussing funeral arrangements. However, thankfully he recovered and the preparations were shelved!

Norman's mother, Grace Alice Symonds, was an only child. Her father was a farmer on the Norfolk-Suffolk border, living in Ellesmere House at Wortham. As a young boy Norman spent nearly as much time at Ellesmere House with his maternal grandparents as at Woodbridge. Both were marvellous places. Ellesmere had a large garden with two greenhouses, one known as 'The Fernery' which was full of green plants. The garden had all kinds of fruit, flowers and a wonderful rubbish heap. Always inquisitive and practical (attributes that were to stand him in good stead in later life), Norman used to spend hours picking mysterious objects out of the rubbish heap, such as bottles and containers with odd liquids in them, all full of interest. He would find further uses for many of them.

Norman was an only child. His mother was an invalid from the earliest time he can remember. Suffering from colitis she had been a patient of Sir William Arbuthnot Lane who performed several large operations on her. Norman commented that over the years Sir William seemed to have removed most of what could have been removed from her abdomen without killing her! Arbuthnot Lane was the preeminent London surgeon of the late Victorian and Edwardian period, and a close friend of Sir Almroth Wright, Alexander Fleming's mentor. Despite her illnesses and many operations Grace lived to the age of 76. However, if Norman ever contracted an infectious illness his mother was always worried about catching it herself and would send Norman to sleep in the summerhouse.

As a boy Norman was an enthusiastic dinghy sailor on the River Deben, an experience that gave him a lifelong love of sailing. Rising in Debenham in Suffolk, the river passes through Norman's hometown of Woodbridge before it turns into a tidal estuary and enters the North Sea at Felixstowe Ferry. Tide Mills at Woodbridge have operated along the River Deben since at least 1170. The present mill, built in 1793, continues to produce stone ground wholemeal flour in the traditional way and would have been a familiar sight to Norman throughout his childhood. The estuary is an area of outstanding natural beauty and Norman would have enjoyed its population of over-wintering avocets, its shifting sandbanks and the widest range of salt marsh flora in Suffolk.

Norman as a Sea Scout

At Woodbridge there was no electricity or gas in the house, and an enormous hand-pump delivered the water from a deep well. It took two men to work the pump and all the water had to be carried by bucket. As a small child Norman remembered having a cosy bath in front of the kitchen range during cold weather.

The main gardener was an elderly gentleman called Crown, although his real name was Wilby. He was called Crown because it was said that he worked for half-a-crown a week until on one occasion he said to Norman's father, "I think I'm worth a crown now."

His grandfather had a chauffeur called Willoughby who drove an American Maxwell car. Coming back late one night his grandmother saw a wheel ahead of them in the headlights. Willoughby saw this too and as he applied his brakes there was a great lurch – one of the wheels had come off the car and was running ahead of them! However, they all managed to return safely and the wheel was eventually fixed.

As a young boy during World War One, Norman remembered seeing the Zeppelins overhead, from which one or two bombs were dropped on Woodbridge. A green warning light would be put in the windows of all the public houses and the wardens would come round saying, "Zeps are out, Zeps are out." Then all the lights had to be put out.

One of his father's favourite phrases was "What are you best at today?", a Suffolk term meaning "What are you planning to do today?" If Norman had no answer he would often say "You go to Mr Sheldrick, and spend an hour or two with him and see what you can pick up." Mr Sheldrick was a toothless old man who made a living soldering broken objects such as old metal teapots, and he would show Norman how to mend these. Norman's daughter also remembers him saying that on other days he might shadow a man working in leather, or learn china riveting from one of the very few people who still knew the art. He would watch the local blacksmith and also learnt how to blow glass. Later in life he would occasionally blow glass at home over a Bunsen burner to show his children how it was done. Unbeknown to him at the time, all these skills would play their part in his future work.

School Days

At the age of six Norman was sent to St Felix School, Southwold, which he thought was 'dreadful', and the nearest thing to William Golding's *Lord of the Flies* that he was ever likely to come across. Originally a good school on the Suffolk coast, it was moved inland to Ipswich during the First World War due to the unlikely prospect of it being bombarded by a German submarine. Here, in a large house in the country with spacious grounds, Norman said that "The teaching was appalling, the food terrible, the supervision poor and the heating non-existent." Norman used to go to bed with a tiny oil lamp, and every evening throughout the influenza pandemic of 1918 he was made to gargle with permanganate of potash.

He spent only one year at that school, when he developed bronchitis and was moved on the advice of a doctor who suggested to his parents that they send him to a school on the south coast. Norman entered Westbourne House in Folkestone, which changed his life. He loved the school, for here he found both an inspirational teacher in Mr Ullyatt, and a life-long school friend by the name of Christopher Morcom. Between the ages of eight and ten these two intelligent boys shared a fascination for everything to do with science, electricity and mechanics.

All the teaching at the school was very good, but the crowning glory was the weekly visit of Mr Ullyatt, an elderly man who used to come to the school to teach science. Although he had a very idiosyncratic way of teaching, the students were enchanted by his lectures. Every week the boys had to write letters home and Norman explained that at least half of the boys would describe what Mr Ullyatt had taught in his last lecture, even before they mentioned the school's football results.

The man combined a conjuror's charisma with his chemistry teaching. He would freeze solutions and make others boil, and he would ignite a mixture of sugar and potassium chlorate by dropping on a single drop of sulphuric acid. He also brought some 'Rupert's Drops', small glass drops that had great internal tensions and slender tails – when the tails were broken off, the whole glass drop would disintegrate into a powder. It was all tremendously inspiring. One magic experiment Norman particularly remembered was when Mr Ullyatt took a large container of water and then added a minute speck of eosin dye. As the pupils watched, it whirled slowly downwards into skeins of beautiful fluorescent pink.

Christopher Morcom was Norman's greatest friend. For some reason (perhaps his mother's chronic illness) Norman's parents did not visit him at boarding school, but Christopher Morcom's parents took both boys out and in the holidays Norman often stayed at their home. Norman was impressed with Mrs Morcom, for as well as having trained as a sculptor at the Slade School, she was very knowledgeable about science, something unusual for women in the 1920s and '30s. She was the daughter of Joseph Swan, co-inventor of the incandescent lamp with Thomas Edison, and very different from Norman's mother who confined her interest to domestic subjects.

Norman's description of his mother was that she was an expert in turning the sides of a worn sheet to the middle using a sewing machine, and in making rice puddings! Norman's frugality and self-sufficiency probably came from his mother and, although in his later life he was very much a family man, he was also happy alone – he once described a very happy Christmas he spent by himself! Norman's wife, Mercy, was to be very thankful for Mrs Morcom's education, as it liberated her from the conventional model of a domestic wife and mother. In fact, Mercy was so poorly equipped for the domestic side of marriage (due to both her boarding school education and her academic ambition) that Norman encouraged her to take cooking lessons before their wedding.

Christopher Morcom and Norman used to invent machines. One was called the 'Waterlandsea', which was a vehicle that could go on or under the water, or on land. Norman would make drawings of this and talk at great length about them when on walks with Christopher. In the early 1920s Norman and Christopher built a crystal radio set together. He recalled:

We seemed to be on the same wavelength and we bounced ideas backwards and forwards. He was such a compassionate person. I went to stay with his family for three weeks at one stage when my mother was having an operation. They lived in a big house called 'The Clockhouse' at Bromsgrove with a big garden and we did not leave the house and garden once in three weeks. We used to do quite a bit of reading in the little nest we built in the wisteria, which was trained over a garden arch. You could climb up the sides of the arch and get into this little nest. We had breakfast and supper on our own but we did have lunch with the family and this was a marvellous education with interesting guests and conversation akin to that in an Oxford or Cambridge senior common room. Christopher was a very clever boy. He was particularly good at mathematics and in one particular term got all the sums right except one where he had added in the date by mistake.

In 1924 Norman left to go to Tonbridge School and it was here that his interest in science was consolidated. He also joined the Signal Corps at school, which had the double benefit of allowing him to avoid parades but also to learn Morse code. He used to practise this on the London Underground, transmitting in Morse the various advertisements on the train. He commented later in life that he still practised this because there was nothing else to do on tube trains! On one occasion he discovered a range finder among the curious collection of military equipment at school. Nobody had the faintest idea how this worked, but Norman examined it, found how it worked and managed to avoid several more parades by demonstrating his expertise with it. Using this piece of equipment he could measure the range of the powder mills and factory chimneys which were two or three miles away from the school.

Back in Woodbridge during the vacations there was another man who had an important influence on the young Norman. Canon Wilkinson had moved to a house behind the family home. He was an eccentric English clergyman who had been a naval padre, but as well as looking after the spiritual needs of the ship he was serving on he had also enjoyed a lot of photographic and radio work, thus maintaining his interest in radio when the First World War was over.

Norman used to enjoy his sermons, which whilst rather quirky were appealing, and he once said to the Canon, "Do you think you could come and preach at Tonbridge? We love having eccentric preachers." Apparently this greatly amused him and he took it in good heart. In his early teens, Norman would often visit Wilkinson and he would greet Norman with, "Hello professor. Do you know how to make hinges?" If Norman said, "No," he would say, "Right, come along to the workshop and I'll show you." And so he did.

Canon Wilkinson's house and garden were full of all kinds of fascinating gadgets, including one that allowed him to do target practice with a revolver from his study window by means of a bar hinged at one end to the top of a three-foot post. To the other end of the bar was fixed a rope which went through a pulley at the top of a six-foot post, then coming back to the study. By this means he was able to control a little model man on a motorcycle who would run up and down the bar, and so enable him to shoot at a moving target.

There was another fascinating object that Norman was shown in Canon Wilkinson's house – the head of Oliver

Cromwell, which he kept in an oak box under his bed. It was a walnut-coloured dark brown head with a wart over the eyebrow. Later in life Norman took his daughter Rose, then aged about 10, and son Christopher, to see this 'head'. The story of Cromwell's head is documented in Appendix 3.

There was one other connection which the Heatleys had with Cromwell. A few doors along from their house in Old Marston was 17b Mill Lane where Cromwell had been based when the Royalists surrendered to the Parliamentarians in 1646. (It is uncertain as to whether or not Cromwell stayed there but he certainly visited the house.)

Cambridge
At school Norman took the entrance examination for Cambridge. He was successful and entered St John's College in Michaelmas Term 1929 where he studied Natural Sciences. He was hoping that Christopher Morcom would join him the following year but that was not to be. At Sherborne School Christopher had became a close friend of Alan Turing and played an influential role in Turing's life. Turing was later to become the 'father' of the computer and during World War Two was based at Bletchley Park where he was involved in breaking the German Enigma code. He was largely responsible for the automatic computing engine (ACE), which was built in Manchester after the war. Turing and Morcom were both brilliant scientists.

In Andrew Hodges' biography of Alan Turing, *The Enigma*, he describes the time when Christopher Morcom and Alan Turing went to Cambridge to sit the entrance examination, adding, "They also went to the cinema together, joined by Norman Heatley, who had been Christopher's friend at preparatory school, and was now a Cambridge undergraduate."

Christopher won a Trinity scholarship in mathematics but sadly never matriculated at Cambridge, dying on Thursday

13th February 1930 after two operations and six days of pain. He suffered from tuberculosis that had afflicted him throughout his school days, having swallowed some infected cows' milk as a small boy. Turing's reaction after Christopher died was such that he said to Mrs Morcom, "I worshipped the ground he stood on." Both Norman at St John's and Alan Turing (who subsequently won a mathematical scholarship to King's College) sorely missed the company of their close friend as a fellow undergraduate.

The Heatleys later named their first son after Christopher, and even into his nineties Norman had a picture of Christopher Morcom on the wall opposite his bed.

At Cambridge Norman's supervisor was Joseph Needham, an unusual scientist who had dedicated himself to the study of Chinese science, culture and history. In his peer group were Dorothy Hodgkin and Derek Richter. Dorothy Hodgkin moved back to Oxford in 1934 when she was appointed to a research fellowship at Somerville College. In Oxford she later went on to confirm the chemical structure of penicillin. This, together with her work on the structure of insulin and vitamin B12, resulted in the award of the Nobel prize in medicine and physiology in 1964. To date she remains Britain's only female Nobel Prize winner in science. Dorothy Hodgkin was Margaret Thatcher's tutor when she (as Margaret Roberts) was an undergraduate at Oxford. Derek Richter became a neuro-scientist and one of the founding fathers of brain chemistry.

After graduating in Natural Sciences with an upper second in 1933, Norman secured a Department of Scientific and Industrial Research grant and joined Gowland Hopkins's laboratory to work on his doctorate for three years, completing his PhD in 1936. His thesis was entitled "The application of micro-chemical methods to biological problems."

Hopkins's laboratory was an extraordinary place. Hopkins himself had been awarded the Nobel Prize for Medicine in 1929 with Christian Eijkman, for their work suggesting there were small molecules essential for animal growth and survival. These hypothetical substances he called 'accessory food factors', but were later renamed vitamins. Working alongside Norman in the laboratory were Ernst Chain, Richard Synge, Frederick Sanger, Hans Krebs and Archer Martin, all of whom subsequently won Nobel prizes.

Chapter 4: Oxford

In 1936, as Norman was coming to the end of his PhD, Chain (who was now working with Florey) asked him on Florey's behalf if he would come to Oxford. It was here in the Sir William Dunn School of Pathology (see Appendix 1) that he was to spend the rest of his working life as a biochemist.

Howard Florey was the youngest of five children, the only boy. Born in Adelaide in 1898 he qualified in medicine in 1921 and came to Oxford as a Rhodes Scholar at Magdalen College in January 1922. Here he came under the influence of Charles Sherrington, an English neurophysiologist and subsequent Nobel laureate, who held the Waynflete Chair of Physiology. He convinced Florey of the importance of physiology as an introduction to pathological research and took him on as a demonstrator in the department.

Florey started his research in Oxford but moved to Cambridge in 1924, after having acted as Medical Officer on an Oxford University Expedition to the Arctic for three months that year. In 1925 he was awarded a Rockefeller Fellowship to the United States. The Rockefeller family had made one of the world's largest fortunes in the oil business in the United States during the late nineteenth and early twentieth centuries and gave a huge amount away to good causes, especially in the field of medicine.

In the USA Florey made important contacts which were to be of great value to him during the development of penicillin. He returned to a Freedom Fellowship at the London Hospital

The Dunn School, Oxford

in September 1926 and the next month he married Ethel Hayter Reed, with whom he had been conducting a courtship by post for five years. Florey soon became disillusioned with the London Hospital, and since Cambridge was still offering him a research post he moved back there in September 1926. He finally completed his PhD in 1927 by which time he had become a Fellow and Director of Medical Studies at Gonville and Caius College.

The next few years strengthened his reputation, and when the Chair of Pathology in Sheffield was advertised in 1931 he decided to apply for it. Despite some professionals saying that "There is no pathologist called Florey," he was elected to the chair and moved to Sheffield in March 1932. His ultimate ambition was achieved in 1935 when he returned to Oxford as Professor of Pathology and Fellow of Lincoln College.

Ernst Chain was born in Berlin in 1906. After the Nazis came to power, Chain knew that he, being Jewish, would no longer be safe in Germany. He left Germany and moved to England, arriving on 2 April 1933 with £10 in his pocket. Geneticist and physiologist JBS Haldane helped him obtain a position at University College Hospital London. After a couple of months he was accepted for a PhD in Cambridge and joined Gowland Hopkins's laboratory. In 1935 Florey, having recently taken up the chair of Pathology in Oxford, sought Hopkins' advice on recruiting a biochemist. Hopkins recommended Chain who duly moved to Oxford in August 1935 to work with Florey.

A few months later Florey again asked Hopkins for possible recruits and this time he recommended Heatley. His reference included:

> *Heatley worked in this department for 3 years and I came to realise that he is a man of marked scientific ability with an experimental skill which is, I believe, greater than any I have ever met.*

Soon afterwards Heatley's PhD supervisor, Joseph Needham, recommended Heatley for an award with the words:

> *Heatley stands quite outside the more ordinary categories of young research workers. From the very beginning of his career he showed that special aptitude for micro-chemical manipulation which has characterised all his work, together with a most unusual flair for the construction of delicate apparatus. I might also refer to the ultra micro-respirometer, highly ingenious and beautiful, which he perfected after his removal from Cambridge to Oxford and has since been applied with collaborators to pathological problems.*

Initially Heatley worked for Chain examining the metabolism of tumours, as Florey was away in Australia for six months. This involved making specialised instruments (referred to above) to measure oxygen, and Heatley's instruments proved to be much more sensitive than the ones that were available at the time. When Heatley decided to publish his work on the new instrument Chain insisted on being a co-author, even though he had made no intellectual or practical contributions to the work. This infuriated Norman and was one of the earliest reasons why he decided he could not continue to be supervised by Chain.

Sadly Chain was one of the very few people (perhaps the only person) that Heatley could not get on with. Their personalities were as chalk and cheese – one dominant, Teutonic, excitable and hierarchical, the other quiet, modest, but courteous. In an interview with Professor Max Blythe in 1987, Heatley explained the reason.

> *I knew him (Chain) slightly at Cambridge and I'm always very grateful to him for getting me to Oxford,*

but we weren't really temperamentally suited. When my term was up at the Dunn School after three years, I was offered a Rockefeller Fellowship to work in Copenhagen with Linderstrom, Lang and Holter, but of course the war came – that was September 1939, and Florey asked me if I would stay on and help him design apparatus. That was something I jumped at, but then I said, "Well look, I don't think I can accept if it means working with Chain," and he said, "Well, that's all right, you will be responsible to me, nobody else." And so I was delighted. I think we (Chain and I) were temperamentally unsuited. Chain had been brought up in the German tradition where you obeyed commands, clicked your heels and said, "Yes sir." And he wanted, I think, to work the same way. He wanted absolute obedience from his people. No, perhaps that is untrue because he did work with others quite amiably and quite satisfactorily, but we spent such a lot of time arguing about things which shouldn't have been discussed and it was a bad relationship at the end.

The importance of his escape from Chain's supervision is illustrated well by a single page from his lab notebook for 1939. The pages of the notebook are generally filled full with writing but p.33 simply has two entries:

Sept 3rd   War declared by Great Britain against
*   Germany*
Oct 1st   Work began with Professor Florey

As stated in the Introduction, these two events seemed to hold a similar significance for Norman.

The difficulty in the relationship between Chain and Heatley continued to present considerable problems as it was essential that Heatley and Chain collaborate during the

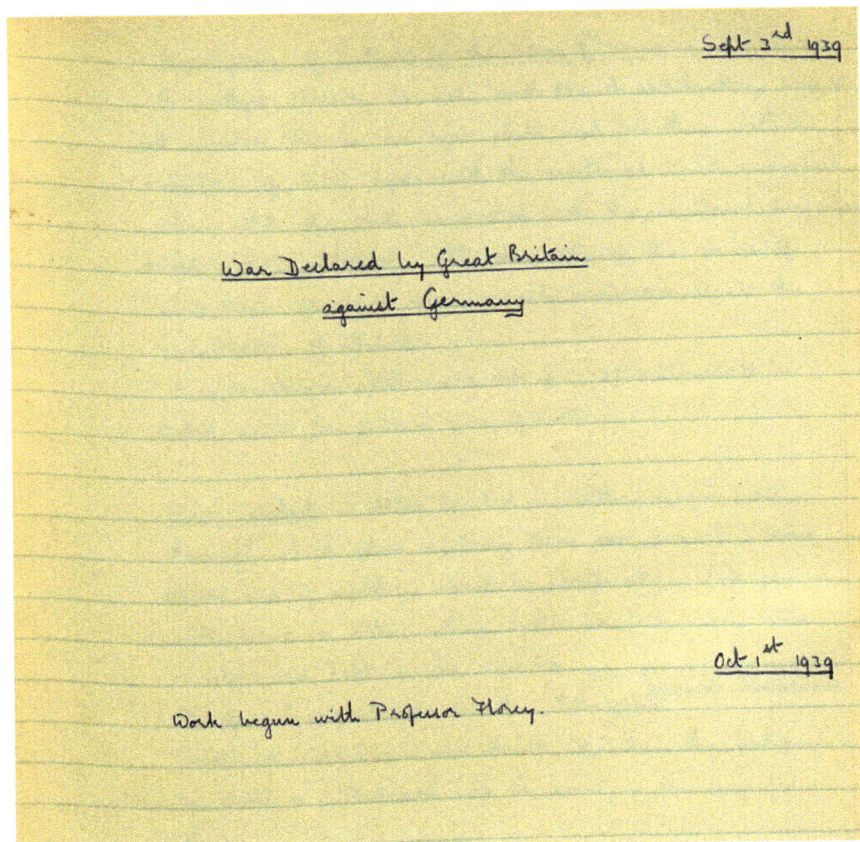

Sept 3rd 1939

War Declared by Great Britain against Germany

Oct 1st 1939

Work begun with Professor Florey.

Heatley's diary entry for 3rd September 1939

penicillin project. Edward Abraham, a fellow biochemist and member of Florey's team, had on many occasions to act as go-between spokesman. One notable disagreement was that Chain insisted that penicillin was yellow and Heatley said, "It may be but we do not know that". It was later found that the impurities were yellow, pure penicillin is white. Norman's daughter Tamsin remembers him at home mimicking Chain: "Heatley I tell you, you are wrong, wrong, wrong!" But on the colour of penicillin Heatley was certainly right.

In 1935, while in Gowland Hopkins's laboratory, Heatley attended a 'Tea Club' lecture on selective enzyme inhibitors. In the discussion afterwards the lecturer was asked if any other selective inhibitors were known. The answer included "Penicillin, a curious fungal product described by Alexander Fleming." Heatley's curiosity was aroused and he took some trouble to consult Fleming's now famous paper of 1929 in the *British Journal of Experimental Pathology* and make notes on it, so when Florey spoke to him in 1939 for the first time about penicillin Norman knew what he was talking about.

The problem that had defeated Fleming and his colleagues was that there was no simple way to extract and purify the penicillin from the culture fluid or to measure its activity. Again and again Florey said to Chain that there had to be a way to get it out and keep it effective. On one occasion, when Heatley was listening quietly, he half apologetically suggested that if penicillin passed from water to ether only when the water was made acid, perhaps it would pass back from ether to water if the water was made alkaline – a chemical 'yo-yo' effect. Chain was unconvinced by what would later be described as a laughably simple idea.

However, Florey was intrigued and set Heatley to work, hoping that he might find appropriate conditions under which penicillin was stable. Heatley achieved this and, having done so, he applied a multi-stage technique to isolate it from the culture fluid and to concentrate it. This realisation that penicillin could be extracted from acidified broth into ether and then extracted back into water held at pH 7 was the key step to the purification process. Heatley's tireless energy in pursuit of the necessary equipment to enable the scaling up of the penicillin production at The Dunn School, together with his innovative ideas, helped increase the momentum generated by Florey and the rest of the team.

As already reported, Heatley's genius for improvisation and invention was apparent from an early age and had been developed in the workshops and garden sheds of his friends and mentors during his formative years. These gifts now became crucial to the purification and production of penicillin and allowed an automated production, using a 'Heath Robinson' set-up of bath, milk churns, petrol cans, biscuit-tins and yards of glass and rubber tubing. The problems of purification were exacerbated in 1939 by the difficulties imposed by wartime restrictions on manufacturing, which meant that Heatley had little or no access to purpose-made apparatus. This forced him to improvise with great ingenuity and make do with everyday objects. He also devised a new assay method that precisely measured the activity of penicillin, in what became known as 'Oxford units'. He was certainly the right man, in the right place, at the right time.

Heatley also played a key role with Florey in the first experiments during May 1940, which demonstrated the remarkable power of penicillin to cure infected animals. He summarised the crucial experiment on Saturday May 25th 1940 in his lecture in 1989 at the Rockefeller University in New York entitled 'Penicillin and Luck' (see Appendix 2).

> *Eight mice were each given a lethal intra-peritoneal injection of virulent streptococci. One hour later, two were given, subcutaneously, a single dose of ten milligrams of a penicillin preparation. Two others were given five milligrams then and four further doses, each of five milligrams, at 3, 5, 7, and 11 hours after infection. The other four mice, the controls, received no penicillin. About 7 hours later the controls looked very sick and died between 13 and 17 hours after infection. All the treated mice looked relatively well. Those receiving the single dose survived for four and six days, while of those receiving the larger, divided dose one died after six days and the other remained well until killed some weeks later.*

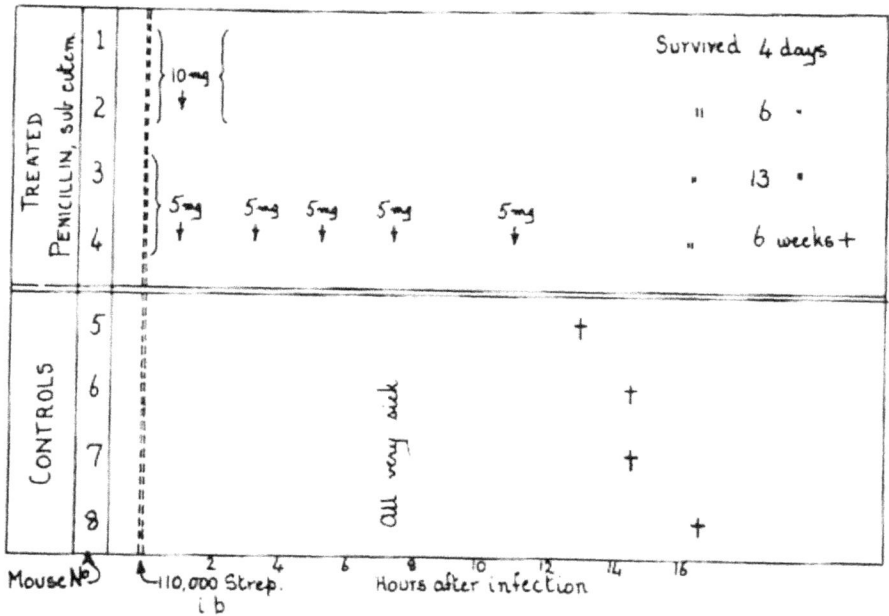

Heatley's hand-drawn diagram of this experiment

This was most encouraging and the next day, a Sunday,
future plans were discussed.

In meticulous handwriting, Heatley recorded the process in
his diary:

After supper with some friends, I returned to the lab and
met the Professor to give a final dose of penicillin to two
of the mice. The 'controls' were looking very sick, but the
two treated mice seemed very well. I stayed at the lab
until 3.45am, by which time all four control animals
were dead.

Typically low key, Heatley's diary entry merely notes that
when he got home, he discovered that he had put his

underpants on back to front in the dark, adding: "It really looks as if penicillin may be of practical importance."

Rev Paul Rimmer, the vicar of Old Marston, also recounts that Norman had told him how on that remarkable night he was riding back with dimmed lights on his bicycle in the blackout days of the war, singing at the top of his voice, having just seen the results of this crucial experiment. He was accosted by a policeman who thought he was drunk, but fortunately Norman managed to persuade him that that was not the case.

Mindful of the threat of a German invasion, Heatley always enjoyed describing how Florey and several of his team impregnated their jackets with *Penicillium* spores, "in case the German tanks came rolling down Headington Hill." This would have enabled them to recover the *Penicillium* and carry on the work elsewhere. This inspired the title of Eric Lax's book on Penicillin published in 2004, *The Mould in Dr Florey's Coat*.

After the results of experiments on mice were published in *The Lancet*, on 24th August 1940, Fleming contacted Florey and visited Oxford to learn more about the breakthrough. It was a surprise to Chain, who is reputed to have said that he thought Fleming was dead. St Mary's Hospital, where Fleming was based, realised the enormous publicity value of their link with penicillin. Charles Wilson (soon to be ennobled as Lord Moran), the Dean at St Mary's and Churchill's physician, together with Lord Beaverbrook, press baron and one-time cabinet minister, and Almroth Wright, Fleming's boss and a London socialite, were all prominent in encouraging the press to publicise and exaggerate the contribution of Fleming and St Mary's Hospital, playing down the importance of the Oxford work. Florey himself must bear some responsibility for the distorted stories put out by the media, because he consistently refused to speak to them and forbade his colleagues to do so. Thus the association of Fleming's name with penicillin was permanently established.

Florey hated any publicity, and feared that desperate relatives of dying patients would plague Heatley and the other team members if news got out of the progress they were making.

After the mouse trials it was clear that a trial of treatment in human patients was urgently needed. However, as Florey pointed out, a human is 3,000 times larger than a mouse, and the amount needed to treat humans was considerably greater. The other problem they faced was that after extraction and purification the dry powder produced was still less than one per cent pure, although it was nevertheless deemed suitable for a clinical trial.

In order to increase production, Norman, always inventive, pressed into service all kinds of laboratory glassware, bottles and containers, some of which he found on Oxford rubbish dumps. It was his idea that ceramics could take the place of the prohibitively expensive glass culture vessels. This led him to use porcelain bedpans from the Radcliffe Infirmary, which proved to be very effective. However, few were available, so Heatley set about designing his own version which became known as the 'penicillin bedpan'. Again good fortune favoured the team, as Florey had a colleague in the potteries who recommended the firm of James MacIntyre in Burslem. They quickly made three ceramic bedpans to Heatley's design – on testing these were entirely satisfactory, and so 500 were ordered. Heatley borrowed a van, drove to the potteries on December 22nd 1940, returned to Oxford with 174 vessels on the 23rd, cleaned and sterilised them on the 24th, and inoculated them with *Penicillium* spores on Christmas day morning. The cultures grown in these vessels, and the several hundred more subsequently obtained from Burslem, turned the

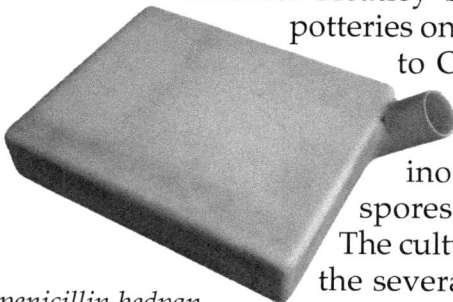

A penicillin bedpan

Oxford laboratory into a virtual penicillin factory. Six 'penicillin girls' were soon employed to assist with 'farming' the cultures.

The Penicillin Girls, with stacked bedpans

CHAPTER 5: THE FIRST PATIENT

By January 1941 it was decided that the 'Dunn School factory' had produced enough crude penicillin to test it on human patients. The Nuffield Professor of Medicine, Leslie Witts, was approached for his advice on choice of appropriate patients. Witts recommended Dr Charles Fletcher, a young Nuffield Research student who had recently finished his house jobs and happened to call into Witts office while Florey was there. Fletcher was looking for a research project and Witts turned to Florey and said, "Here's your man, Fletcher can do the testing."

It was decided that a toxicity test was first required, as the side effects on humans were unknown and could possibly have had fatal consequences. Mrs Elva Akers, a lady with terminal cancer, agreed to be the 'guinea pig'. There were no ethical committees then and no other permission was needed. She received a 100mgm injection of penicillin and two hours later had a rigor (a shivering attack with high temperature). This meant that the penicillin preparation contained some impurities (pyrogens). Edward Abraham, who had recently joined the team, suggested that chromatography should be introduced into the isolation procedures and this helped remove the pyrogenic materials.

It had become clear that penicillin could not be given by mouth, as it would not survive passage through the stomach. Tests of intravenous, intramuscular and rectal routes showed that intravenous injection was best. In early February 1941 Fletcher, in discussion with Florey, found the worst case of sepsis in the Radcliffe Infirmary. The patient was a 43-year-old local policeman from Abingdon by the name of Albert Alexander who had a staphylococcal and streptococcal infection resistant to large doses of sulphapyridine (the best drug available at that time). He became the first human patient to be treated systemically with an intravenous injection of penicillin. He had been in hospital for two months and the infection had spread to his scalp. An abscess there had spread to both his eyes, one of which had had to be removed. He had open abscesses on his arm, as well as abscesses in his lungs, and was well on his way towards death from the terrible overwhelming infection.

It is interesting that there are two quite different accounts of how he acquired the infection. One says simply that he scratched his face on a rose thorn in his garden. The second says that he was injured in a bombing raid on a police station in Southampton, where he had been posted. Whichever is true, he was very close to death, "Oozing pus everywhere and in great pain" when he received his first injection of 200 milligrams on February 12th. This was followed up by 100 milligrams every three hours.

The plaque at the entrance of the Old Radcliffe Infirmary

After 24 hours he had made a dramatic improvement, and by the fourth day he was able to take lunch at the table in the centre of the ward. Since the kidneys excrete much of the administered penicillin, his urine was collected and returned to the Dunn School where the penicillin was re-extracted, taken back to the Radcliffe Infirmary and re-injected into the patient. Despite this recycling, supplies were low, and after five days of intensive treatment little penicillin remained. Since Alexander was much better, it was decided to stop treatment. He held his own for about ten days but then slowly succumbed to the infections and died about a month later.

Fletcher would cycle from the Radcliffe Infirmary to the Dunn School each evening with bottles of the patient's urine for penicillin extraction and re-use. Over the next four months from February to June 1941, Fletcher treated further patients with penicillin. Some were children to whom smaller doses could be given. The first of these was a boy of 15 who was near death with septicaemia, acquired from an infected hip wound following hip surgery. Within two days he was much improved and remained well, and a month later was able to have the pin removed from his hip. Another case Fletcher described as one of the most memorable moments of his career was when he treated, in May 1941, a boy of four with a cavernous sinus thrombosis (in the brain) due to infection. He describes the boy's cat-like wailing cries from the pain, which ceased after his treatment. Sadly the boy died a week later of a brain haemorrhage following rupture of a weak blood vessel, but the penicillin effect was astounding – there was no sign of infection in the boy's brain at post-mortem examination.

The results were published in *The Lancet* in August 1941. Florey and his team soon realised the effect that penicillin could have on the outcome of the war, and made plans to increase production as rapidly as possible. However, increasing the yield of the batches of antibiotic was impossible

The Radcliffe Infirmary

without industrial-scale production, and the major British pharmaceutical companies were unable to help as they needed to focus on drugs which were already tried and tested for the war effort.

USA

Florey had realised that the chances of getting industry involved might be greater in the USA than in Britain. Having previously worked in America and also having befriended some American Rhodes Scholars in Oxford, he had valuable contacts there which quickly began to pay dividends. Florey obtained approval for a USA visit from the Medical Research Council and the appropriate United States authorities. The Rockefeller Foundation provided the funds for the trip. He decided to take Heatley with him, since it was he who knew most about growing the mould and extracting the antibiotic. These plans were secret and Chain only learnt about them an hour before Florey and Heatley set out. Chain was furious, thinking that it was he, not Heatley, who should have accompanied Florey. It was probably this event more than any other which soured relations between Chain and Florey, and they never really recovered.

Accordingly, in late June 1941 Heatley accompanied Florey to the USA on a transatlantic flight. This was a potentially perilous journey with a real possibility of being shot down by German fighter planes. Florey and Heatley drove to Bristol on 26th June where they spent the night at The Grand Hotel, and at 7.00am the following morning were driven to Whitchurch airfield from where they took off for Lisbon in a blacked-out plane via an undisclosed route that included a stop at an unidentified airfield. At Lisbon Rockefeller's representatives took care of all formalities, although the pair had to wait four days before they boarded the clipper flight to New York via the Azores and Bermuda, arriving on the afternoon of 2nd July. In anticipation of such an event, Heatley had (as had become his practice) rubbed spores of the *Penicillium* species into the seams of his overcoat, so that there would be a chance of the penicillin-producing mould being recovered if and when his corpse was found.

Florey's ambitious plan was to obtain one kilogram of pure penicillin. After discussions with various senior American scientists it was agreed that they should consult Charles Thom, a leading mycologist (mould expert). He recommended a visit to the US Department of Agriculture's Research Laboratory in Peoria, Illinois. This laboratory was expert in the large-scale manufacture of chemicals by fermentation. A collaboration was quickly agreed and Heatley was assigned to work with Dr AJ Moyer, who suggested adding corn-steep liquor (a by-product of starch extraction) to the growth medium. With this and other subtle changes – such as using lactose in place of glucose, and isolating a higher-yielding strain of *Penicillium* from a mouldy melon found (after a worldwide search) in the local market – they were able to push up yields of penicillin to 20 units per ml. However, their cooperation had become one-sided, and Heatley noted that, "Moyer had begun not telling me what he was doing."

Florey returned to Oxford in September. On 9th Oct 1941 he wrote to Heatley in typical Florey fashion:

> *As far as I can see things are much the same here, although the production of penicillin is apparently in a complete state of chaos.*
>
> *I have succeeded Chain in the brewing department and told the girls to go on just making one brew and then starting again, there should at least be some supplies of material.*
>
> *There doesn't seem to be much else of interest as the department seems to be semi-moribund as far as I can see.*

Heatley stayed on in Peoria until December, and for the next six months he worked at Merck & Co in Rahway, New Jersey. In July 1942 he returned to Oxford and was soon to learn why Moyer had become so secretive. When Moyer published their research results, he omitted Heatley's name from the paper, despite an original contract which had stipulated that any publications should be jointly authored. Fifty years on, Heatley confessed that he was amused, rather than upset, by Moyer's duplicity. Later he was to learn that financial greed had led Moyer to claim all the credit for himself. To have acknowledged Heatley's part of the work would have made it difficult to apply for patents with himself as sole inventor, which is what he did.

Florey had earlier been advised by University lawyers and the Medical Research Council that he should not take out patents on his team's discoveries. Chain disagreed strongly with this advice and tried very hard to change it. He had, after all, come from a German background where new discoveries were usually patented.

The United States collaboration had made it possible to produce sufficient amounts of penicillin to treat casualties of the war. The end result of this initiative was that by late 1943 mass production of the drug had begun in America using a deep-tank fermentation process – another major methodological advance which increased yields very significantly.

In May 1943, Florey travelled to North Africa with Professor Hugh Cairns, the Nuffield Professor of Surgery in Oxford and a pioneer in treating the head injuries of wounded soldiers. He was the surgeon who looked after TE Lawrence (Lawrence of Arabia) following his motorcycle accident from which he was to die, and he pressed for the introduction of motorcycle helmets. They had just enough penicillin to put the drug through the most demanding tests so far, the treatment of war wounds. The results were dramatic and there was no doubt that a new miracle cure had been found. The results made headline news.

However, it also provided an ethical dilemma since it had recently been discovered that penicillin was extremely effective in curing the 'clap' (gonorrhoea). This posed the question – who should get the precious but limited supplies of penicillin? Should seriously wounded soldiers be given it to save their lives, or should fit soldiers who had contracted venereal diseases by their own activities be given it so that, when quickly cured, they could be sent back to fight again. No doctors on the front line could decide. The dilemma was passed all the way up to Churchill. He responded by saying, "This valuable drug must on no account be wasted. It must be used to the best military advantage." This was interpreted to mean that the victims of 'clap' should be treated so that they could be rapidly returned to the front lines.

By 1944, when Allied forces landed on the beaches of Normandy, enough penicillin was available to treat wounded British and American troops. In the United States, as penicillin and other antibiotics became widely used, the number of deaths from major infections began to plummet. At the same time overall life expectancy climbed.

CHAPTER 6: LIFE AFTER PENICILLIN

In 1948, as a result of the work on penicillin, the famous philanthropist and car manufacturer, Lord Nuffield, endowed three research fellowships at Lincoln College. Heatley was elected to one of these, and Edward Abraham and Gordon Sanders, two other members of the penicillin team, to the others. Heatley's relationship with Lincoln College, which continued almost to the end of his life, was a particularly happy one.

After the excitement of penicillin, the rest of his career might well have seemed something of an anti-climax, but his skill in introducing new methods to the laboratory and refining and miniaturizing existing ones remained. The results, many of them in collaboration with a wide range of scientists, were described in more than sixty scientific papers that he wrote or co-authored. His first was "A new type of microburette," another "On drilling small holes in glass," and the seminal penicillin paper on 24th August 1940, "Penicillin as a chemotherapeutic agent," published in the *Lancet*. The last scientific paper recorded in his bibliography was published in the *British Journal of Experimental Pathology* in 1977. Its title was, "On the production of antibodies to staphylococcal delta-lysin in rabbits."

Heatley's Diaries and Lab Notebooks

As already mentioned, Heatley wrote extensively in his personal diaries and in his laboratory notebooks. Fortunately

Lincoln College, Oxford

for posterity these have been preserved and passed on by his family to the archive at the Wellcome Trust. They make fascinating reading and contributed to a much better understanding of Norman as a real-life character.

One of the earliest entries concerned the Heatley family motto, translated from the family crest and passed on by 'Aunt Lil': "They will rise highest who aim at the highest things."

Many of the entries are, in a sense, trivial, concerned with the weather, how Norman slept, how tired he became, what he ate (in the lab, under trees in the University Parks and at restaurants, especially The Taj Mahal!), but they help set the scene and describe what life was really like during the wartime years.

There are many references to searching for 'digs' and sleeping on friends' settees, often that of Gordon Sanders, who clearly had superior digs in Polstead Road. Norman's final digs, from where he married, were at 17 Kingston Rd with Mrs Brooks as his landlady.

Norman was clearly a social animal and many entries refer to friends. He had a number of lady friends including Melissa and Micky before he met Mercy. One touching entry (Oct 8th 1939), about Melissa, asks, "Shall I ever find anyone so good and kind and considerate to me." Apparently he did… but it was not until May 27th 1944 that Norman met Mercy Bing at a Somerville dance. Mercy was a medical student at that college. Norman proposed to Mercy on September 13th 1944, and his diary records the event:

> *This is a very important day for when Mercy came into the Parks and had lunch with me I proposed to her. We sat under the silver birch where I used to eat my lunch when I first came to Oxford; it was exceedingly difficult to put the actual question. Mercy must have known it was coming for she ate hardly any lunch.*

The wedding was a low key affair at Binsey church on Monday, December 18th 1944. The diary records for this period falter. For Thursday, 13th December:

Felt rather queasy today. Supper with Mercy, who had had a very busy day getting the bedroom straight.

The next entry simply reads:

Was married on Dec 18th but forgot to take this diary with me. As I wanted to write while we were still in London Mercy got me another book and I wrote in that, starting on Dec 17th.

The entry for Dec 18th is:

After breakfast packed up a suitcase and took it with the rest of my belongings at 17 Kingston Rd to Mercy's digs. There I left most of the odds and ends and collected her suitcase. Took it and mine down to the station and left them in the left luggage office.......back in my digs I was about to set off for Mercy when she arrived complete with bridal bouquet of anemones and Wilmington myrtle... we then set off for Binsey together. It was a lovely fresh morning and we stopped off on all the bridges to admire the views. We were a few minutes late at the church.... The service was lovely and Mr Barry (the clergyman) did his part so extremely nicely. It was exactly what Mercy and I wanted it to be.

After the service Norman and Mercy walked to a friend's house where a lunch party had been arranged for about 15 people – "the lunch was quite a success."

From this account it appears that neither Norman's nor Mercy's family were at the wedding, although one of the guests was Miles Vaughan Williams, a medical school contemporary of Mercy's who was to become a distinguished pharmacologist and medical tutor. At the time of writing he is still alive and lively, living on the Woodstock Road in Oxford.

After the lunch Norman and Mercy were driven to the station where they caught a train to London.

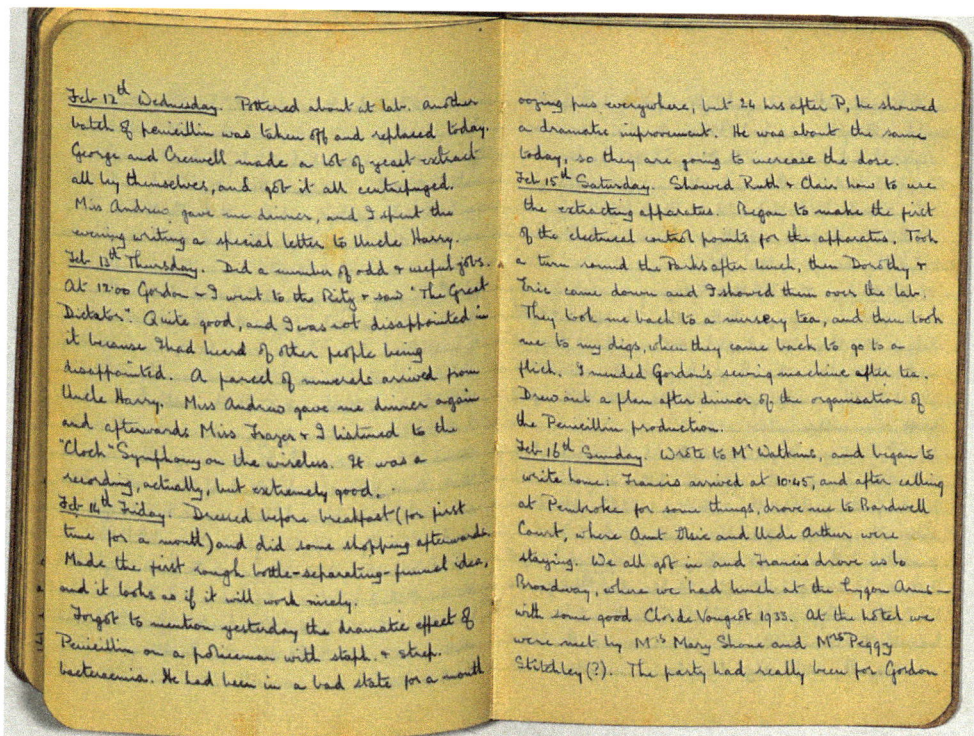

Heatley's diary entry for 14th February 1941,
two days after the first injection of penicillin.

After reporting that he dressed before breakfast, the first time for a month, he then did some shopping and at the lab made a rough bottle-separating funnel which looks as if it will work nicely. He then went on: "forgot to mention yesterday the dramatic effect of penicillin on a policeman with staph & strep bacteraemia. He had been in a bad state for a month oozing pus everywhere, but 24hrs after P he showed a dramatic improvement. He was about the same today, so they are going to increase the dose." The contrast between trivia and momentous events in the diary is startling!

Chapter 7: Home Life

When Norman and Mercy moved into their house in Old Marston in 1946 Norman insisted on the help of au pairs in the family home, many of whom became lifelong friends. They had five children: Rose, Christopher, Piers (who died tragically in an accident at the age of three), Jonathan and Tamsin. Rose was born in hospital but the other four children were born at home with Norman assisting the midwife. On one occasion, when Mercy had used all the oxygen and gas, Norman rushed off to the local GP for an extra cylinder. The valve and other accessories came in 20 parts – Norman carefully studied the small print with Mercy writhing and groaning and fitted it all together successfully for a safe and happy delivery. Not only was Mercy wife to Norman and mother to their children, but she also followed her own career as a child psychiatrist.

Soon after their marriage, while moving into a new home, the removal men assured them that a tall linen press could not be carried up the stairs. "Right," said Norman to Mercy when the furniture movers departed, "Now you and I will carry this up." He skilfully made a cut through this antique cupboard so

OXFORDSHIRE BLUE PLAQUES BOARD

NORMAN HEATLEY
DM
1911-2004
Biochemist
key member of the Oxford
penicillin team 1939-43

lived here
1946-2004

OXFORD CIVIC SOCIETY

St Nicholas Church, Old Marston

carefully that later it was imperceptible, and the press was then easily transported in two pieces!

Norman was a proud and involved husband and father. His rabbit hutches were second-to-none, and he improvised many indoor occupations for the children including slides down the stairs and a 'rock boat' on the landing made from an old pram. He also enjoyed reading stories to the children at bedtime.

Rev Paul Rimmer, the former vicar of Old Marston, recalls his first meeting with Norman in 1959. Paul had taken some of the Sunday school children punting at Magdalen Bridge and saw a boy fall in from a makeshift raft close by. His colleague on the raft shouted for help as the boy could not swim and Paul dived in fully clothed to save him. The description of this under the headline 'Vicar Saves Drowning Boy' appeared in the Oxford papers, and a few days later Norman turned up on the vicar's doorstep and handed him a ten-shilling note saying, "I read about what you did the other day and this will help to get your jacket and trousers cleaned."

On another occasion Paul went into St Nicholas Church to

see a pair of feet lying in the aisle. It looked as if someone had been praying and then collapsed, but he soon discovered that it was Norman lying horizontal to fix one of the broken pews. He often went into the church quietly and fixed anything that was broken. He was generous in all things and thought nothing of allowing Paul and Joan Rimmer the free use of their family house in Wilmington when Paul was recovering from a bad bout of pneumonia.

On one occasion the vicar's son, Julian Rimmer, went with his girlfriend round to Norman and Mercy Heatley's for lunch. They were surprised to find not only that Norman had a bed in his study, but that he was lying on it watching Fred Astaire and Ginger Rogers on the television, two of his favourite stars whom he adored.

Despite a fear of heights, in 1977 Norman volunteered to re-attach the Old Marston church flag to its pole at the top of the tower for the occasion of the Queen's Silver Jubilee. His weight caused the pole to lean over at a disturbing angle, giving great concern to the onlookers who feared it was in imminent danger of breaking and sending Norman crashing to the ground. However, the flag was successfully reattached and he returned safely to terra firma.

Next door to the Heatleys in Old Marston lived Vic and Alice Haynes, an elderly brother and sister in a picturesque, thatched, damp cottage. Norman and Mercy suggested buying their cottage, which they did and then rebuilt it in order to give the Haynes updated accommodation downstairs and provide Mercy Heatley with a consulting room upstairs. After the death of Vic and Alice, the bottom flat was rented out to a succession of DPhil students and their partners. Norman turned their monthly payment of rent into a pleasant ceremony with glasses of exceptionally potent home-made beer. If the partners married and the bride's father was unavailable, Norman gave the bride away. He would also make the wedding punch and convert the fruit left over to delicious marmalade. On one occasion, when a tenant arrived with a large collection of books, Norman made a floor-to-ceiling bookcase for him, fitting it perfectly into the room.

A leaking waterbed provided Norman's most dramatic intervention as a landlord. He had not seen a water-bed before but understood the principle of manufacture. Inserting a hose into the bed he drained the water out of the front door, down the slope and onto the road. It was a period of record drought but fortunately no passer-by saw the flood that gushed out of the house. He was then able to mend the bed and refill it.

Described by one of his friends as a 'generous puritan', Norman could never bring himself to throw anything away. Indeed, he would seek out and examine local rubbish skips for anything that he might find useful in the future. He spent little money on himself – he preferred his old clothes and rode his bicycle for 15 years until he traded it in. The week he did so happened to be Road Safety Week and the shop put his bike in the middle of the window with a notice saying, 'Until yesterday this bicycle was actually being ridden'. Streamers pointed to its dysfunctional handlebars, saddle and pedals.

In Old Marston he was known to be very welcoming to newcomers and a very kind neighbour. On one occasion he was able to pick the front door lock of an elderly confused neighbour who had locked herself out. He was well read and would often ask friends and visitors for book recommendations. He could read well in French as well as in English.

When Raymond Blanc, the well-known chef and restaurant owner, bought the house next door to the Heatleys, Norman made him an apple crumble which he took to welcome him to Old Marston. Years later Mercy saw Raymond at his own restaurant in Walton Street and asked him if he remembered. "Yes," he said. "I was delighted. I had thought of English people as cold and unfriendly. Your husband changed my mind."

Dr Tony Raine, a renal consultant who bought a house in Old Marston in the 1980s, was surprised shortly after he and his wife moved in by a knock on the door. He opened it to see Norman standing there announcing that he was a local resident and had noticed that they had just moved in. He asked if he could do anything to help. Tony had trained in Oxford and had been taught by Norman as an undergraduate. Knowing his medical reputation, he was amazed to see him on his doorstep with screwdriver and hammer in hand.

CHAPTER 8: RETIREMENT

In September every year Norman would travel to the British Association for the Advancement of Science meetings where he would sleep in his Dormobile in a car park. Those to whom he wished to talk would be invited in for tea or coffee. During the free time at these meetings he liked to join one of the local outings to see whatever the local town had to offer. He would select a technical outing to a local factory or laundry and enjoyed sitting next to any person on the coach journey, whether nun or schoolboy, who was passionate about science.

He was an enthusiastic and skilled gardener, training fruit trees into espaliers, grafting one apple species onto another, producing vegetables for the family table or cutting flowers for Lincoln College chapel, or a visiting friend. Such was his love of the garden that he was never keen on taking family holidays, which irked Mercy who would have enjoyed being away a little more often. He built a wall with some of the disused penicillin pans and on another occasion broke others up to make a base for his garden shed. Few now remain, although it is said that Damian Hurst bought one for £14,000!

Norman was in many ways a man ahead of his time. He was happy to use a sewing machine, shorten his shirtsleeves, make a lampshade or pair of curtains; he did the family washing, and on occasions he cooked from his own notebook of recipes. An excellent host, his practical brilliance was matched by his down-to-earth, sometimes impish good humour. He was an excellent raconteur and good company.

For more than 50 years, the Heatleys' home in Marston village was a welcoming haven for generations of students and scientists working in Oxford.

On one occasion his daughter Tamsin was working with 'Lumière and Son Theatre Company'. This fringe production took place in a large circus tent on the lawn of Magdalen College School. At the end of the season Norman watched the actors struggle to take up the deeply embedded tent pegs, which were so heavy it took two people to carry them. They looked politely sceptical when Norman, already frail and elderly, offered to help them. With his own individual and innovative technique he made a special tent peg machine that winched them out by a lever made from bits from his workshop. This allowed them to uproot the heavy pegs with much less effort than the actors had been using.

When *Brideshead Revisited* was being cast, his daughter Tamsin encouraged Norman to apply as an extra. He went along in his best suit. The costume unit inspected this and said with surprise, "But you are perfectly dressed for the thirties." His role was to be an Oxford don strolling across the courtyard with another don. After a short while, deep in apparent discussion, dialogue ran dry. "Tell me about Boyle's Law," suggested the other Don. "The fascinating thing about Boyle's Law," Norman replied, "is that I cannot recall a single thing about it."

Even in his last decade, as his health and memory faded, he never lost his inventive flair. He delighted in making wonderfully delicate miniature furniture from birds' quills, and an exquisite example of this is shown here. After one operation, he insisted on bringing

home from hospital the plastic drip containers, cutting them down to make food containers for the fridge.

David Cranston (one of the authors), a licensed lay minister at Old Marston church, helped Rev Paul Rimmer serve communion on many occasions. Often Margaret Florey and Norman Heatley would be kneeling side-by-side at the Communion rail. On another occasion he asked if Norman had any spare copies of the Florey papers, and was amazed to hear a knock on the door of his house in Yarnton several weeks later and found Norman standing at the door, holding a collection of published papers, all carefully numbered in order of publication.

Eric Sidebottom (the other author) first met Norman Heatley as an undergraduate at The Dunn School in 1960. Later, in 1966, he returned as a DPhil student and became the grateful recipient of Norman's advice and practical help. He noted that Norman never wasted anything, probably due to his experiences of shortages of materials during the war years. He recalls him on one occasion attending a Journal Club taking notes in tiny precise writing with a mapping pen on the inside of a used envelope that he had carefully torn open. Another graduate reported that:

> *His generosity of spirit to younger and considerably more junior colleagues can be illustrated by two examples: Heatley happened to hear a third party grumbling that he had damaged yet another expensive commercial 5µL pipette in the course of his experiments. Norman then proceeded, unasked, to make from glass and rubber tubing a micropipette that he diffidently assured him would accurately dispense exactly 1.32µL. Just before starting at The Dunn School, another graduate had submitted a paper to the* Journal of General Microbiology. *He said, "Shortly after my arrival, Heatley, who was at that time an Editor of that*

journal, a fact of which I was ignorant, spontaneously sought me out to ask my agreement to his redrafting large parts of my text in order to clarify the meaning." Such kind acts towards a junior member of staff were typical of him. He was also an enthusiastic teacher, who took great interest in his pupils: shortly after a practical class in bacteriology numbering about 80 medical students where I had been helping as a Demonstrator, Heatley remarked that he now knew the names of almost all the students, an astonishing achievement considering that we had seen this class on only two previous occasions and that in those days name badges were not used.

Eric Sidebottom goes on to relate the following story:

As my younger son was preparing for his GCSE in history he mentioned to me that they were doing a 'medical history' module which included the story of penicillin. It immediately occurred to me that it might be inspiring for the young students to hear the story from the 'horse's mouth'. Norman readily agreed and gave a modest, understated account of his role to 300 pupils in what I describe as 'The twentieth century's most important medical discovery.' Most of the students realised that they were being 'taught' by someone rather special and they christened him 'Stormin' Norman' after General Norman Schwarzkopf, Commander-in-Chief of the coalition forces in the Gulf War during 1990. It is difficult to imagine a less appropriate name for Norman George Heatley, but it gives a nice indication of how quickly he aroused affection in the people with whom he interacted (apart from Ernst Chain!). For those of us who knew him, the idea of 'Stormin' Norman' quickly brings a smile to our faces.

CHAPTER 9: LEGACY

While Fleming received more than 180 honours (honorary degrees, medals, prizes, decorations, freedom of cities, and honorary memberships of scientific societies and academies – even a crater on the moon was named after him), Heatley received just one honorary degree – from Oxford in 1990. This was an honorary doctorate in medicine, only the second given in Oxford's 800-year history, and the first to a non-medic. In Heatley's view, "an enormous privilege, since I am not medically qualified." He received two honorary fellowships at Lincoln College, Oxford, and St John's College, Cambridge. He was also honoured with an OBE in 1978.

During his lifetime Norman Heatley did not receive the recognition we all now believe he deserved. One example of this is that he was never appointed as a fellow of The Royal Society, Britain's leading, and the world's oldest scientific society, despite being nominated by a very distinguished group of scientists. He was proposed for fellowship in 1958 by HW Florey, EP Abraham, HH Dale, JH Burn, PB Medawar, P Fildes, AG Ogston, Dorothy Hodgkin and JW Cornforth. The citation read:

> *Heatley, Norman George (Old Marston nr Oxford) MA, PhD, Senior Research Officer, University of Oxford. His principal claim to election depends upon his important contributions to the introduction of penicillin into*

Heatley in procession after receiving his DM

medicine. He carried out all the experimental and production fermentation during the first part of the work on penicillin at Oxford and devised the cylinder plate assay for its assay.

This method of assay has been used in the isolation of all the antibiotics now used in medicine and is widely employed for a variety of purposes.

He extended Clutterbuck, Lovell and Raistrick's observations on the extraction of penicillin to a workable solvent-transfer process still used in its manufacture.

Since the work on penicillin he has isolated, described and worked on other antibiotics and is currently working on gastro-intestinal secretion muco-substances and secretin.

Although it is very unusual for a nominee to be elected on the first occasion, their nomination is reconsidered annually until the current rules decree it should lapse. Norman's nomination lapsed in 1967 and was not renewed. We believe the Royal Society missed out on a very deserving fellow.

Those who knew him readily understood why he became the 'unsung hero of penicillin.' He was a most delightful, old-fashioned gentleman; modest to a fault, courteous, kind, considerate, and always looking for ways to help others. He was a team player, rather than a leader of men.

Although he may not have received many public honours, he did have in large measure the enormous satisfaction of knowing that he was a key part of the team that gave the world its first practical antibiotic – one that saved the limbs and lives of thousands of allied troops in the Second World War, and subsequently literally millions of patients all round the world. For generations brought up post-penicillin, it is hard to remember that before antibiotics many infections were lethal. They were feared as cancer and heart disease are today, as has been poignantly described by Mary Soames in her biography of her mother, Clementine Churchill. She describes how in 1921 her young sister developed a sore throat and goes on to say, "The local doctor was very good but the age of antibiotics had not yet dawned, and her painful sore throat progressed into a fatal septicaemia."

Heatley died on 5 January 2004 at his home, 12 Oxford Road, Marston, Oxford. On 15 January his green cardboard coffin, covered with his DM robe, was carried in procession from his home to St Nicholas's Church, Marston, for the funeral service. The church was packed to overflowing, and during the service his recorded voice was heard reading to his children. In death, as in life, Norman Heatley was able to surprise us all.

Heatley with penicillin bed pan and cat

Norman Heatley's name is commemorated in an annual Heatley lecture at Oxford, a graduate scholarship awarded in his name, and by Heatley Road in Oxford Science Park.

Appendix 1: The Dunn School of Pathology

The Dunn School of Pathology was named after Sir William Dunn who had no direct connections with medicine. He belonged to that Victorian generation of Scottish pioneers who went overseas to make their fortunes, and yet devoted the money he made to numerous charitable purposes, mainly at home in the United Kingdom. His family origins were modest – he was born in Paisley, near Glasgow on Sept 1st 1833, the youngest son of John Dunn and Isobella Chalmers, who kept a small shop in Maxwelton Street.

In 1847, at the age of 14, he joined the office of a local accountant, John Muir, with a salary of just £5 per year. In 1852 at the age of 19, and with the encouragement and advice of one of his father's friends, the local MP for Paisley, Mr William Barbour (whom Dunn was to succeed as MP nearly 40 years later), he made the momentous step of emigrating to Port Elizabeth in South Africa. There he joined the merchant trading and importing firm of William Mackie and Co and his abilities were soon recognised – he became a partner when he was 21 and the sole proprietor at the age of 26 on the sudden death of the original owner. He also set up successful companies of his own in Durban (W Dunn & Co), and in East London (Dunn & Co) on returning to England in 1862. Before returning to make his base in London he had married a wealthy South African lady, Sarah Elizabeth Howse. They did not have any children but later adopted William's niece, also Sarah.

Dunn quickly established himself in London as a successful businessman trading with all corners of the world. He bought a house in Kensington and a country estate of 2,000 acres at Lakenheath in Suffolk. Although based in the South of England he never forgot his Scottish origins and made several bequests to Paisley. In 1891 he became the Liberal MP for Paisley, a post he held until 1906.

He died in 1912 with an estate valued at £1.3 million. In his will, dated 4 November 1908, the key clause was 'to advance the cause of Christianity, to benefit children and young people, to support hospitals and alleviate human suffering, to encourage education and promote emigration.' After making provision for half the total, he left the remainder in the hands of his Trustees. They allotted about 120 small sums to hospitals, nursing homes, orphanages and similar institutions, but then decided that larger projects would be more likely to be permanent memorials to Sir William.

After consulting the President of the Royal Society, Sir William Hardy, and the Secretary of the Medical Research Committee, Sir Walter Fletcher, the Trustees gave £210,000 in 1920 to Sir Frederick Gowland Hopkins's Biochemistry Department in Cambridge and £100,000 in 1922 to Professor George Dreyer's Pathology Department in Oxford. This enabled the building of the Dunn School that was opened in 1927. Between them, these two laboratories in Oxford and Cambridge have 'spawned' nine Nobel Prize winners. The 'alleviation of human suffering' achieved would surely have pleased Sir William and his trustees, and no doubt he would be pleased to hear the Dunn School described as "The place where God's work is done," as the following story relates.

A few years ago, after I (Eric Sidebottom) had given a seminar on the 'True Story of Penicillin', an elderly workshop technician came to talk to me. He showed a great interest in the penicillin story and on asking him why he was so interested, he told me that as a child he would often walk past the Dunn School with his mother. She usually stopped outside the gates, turned towards the building, bowed her head and whispered a short prayer. On asking why she did this he was told, "This is the place where God's work is done." His mother explained that her brother (his uncle) was badly wounded in the war and brought back to the Radcliffe Infirmary where it was expected that he would die from his wounds. He was given the last rites of his church. However, Dr Charles Fletcher saw him and gave him penicillin – he recovered.

Appendix 2: Penicillin and Luck: Norman Heatley's Version

In 1989 Norman made a nostalgic return to the USA. Some of the visit was covered by BBC documentary makers and was recorded for posterity. During the visit Norman gave a lecture at The Rockefeller University in New York. His title was 'Penicillin and Luck'. He started by going back 60 years to his time as an undergraduate at Cambridge where on most days he walked past a building on which was engraved the quotation from Louis Pasteur, 'Le hazard ne favourise que ceux qui sont préparer' (Luck only favours those who are prepared). Norman said that he took this aphorism to heart but was equally impressed by Paul Erlich's opinion that successful research requires the four Gs: "geschick (skill), geduld (patience), geld (money), and glück (luck)." Unfortunately, Erlich did not explain how to acquire luck.

Norman then went on to talk about several examples of how 'good luck' had played a part in the early history of penicillin. First he said that his invitation to join Howard Florey's laboratory in Oxford in 1936 was enormously lucky for him. It determined the course of the rest of his life, not only his role in developing penicillin but also his marriage and family, and his role as a 'sage' and much loved long-standing resident of Old Marston.

However, before this the first stroke of luck in the story was that of Alexander Fleming. The mysterious events leading up to the appearance of the famous plate in Fleming's discard tray has been the source of much speculation. The explanations of Ronald Hare in his several publications describing in detail the work in Fleming's laboratory and his own investigations of the phenomenon seem the most likely to be correct. Hare speculates on the likely/necessary sequence of events and the ambient temperatures to which the plate had been exposed during Fleming's holiday absence. The fact that it has not been described again as happening by chance in any laboratory in the world shows how rare a phenomenon it was but makes even more important the event described in Norman's lab notebook when a medical student in the classroom produced a plate showing bacterial antagonism – see Appendix 4.

Heatley next described the situation regarding equipment, especially the difficulties in obtaining new equipment in wartime Britain. In this section there is a charming example of Heatley's modesty. "A minor piece of luck was that one of Florey's team was interested in the art of china riveting and had the necessary equipment for drilling holes in glass." That member was, of course, Heatley himself!

The next piece of luck Heatley describes concerns the 'stackable bedpans' which became the principal culture vessels for the penicillin used for the first human trials in February 1941. After a discouraging response from a major glassware manufacturer to an enquiry about the possibility of designing and manufacturing suitable vessels, Florey contacted a colleague in the potteries and was advised that James MacIntyre of Burslem might be able to help. That story has already been described.

Perhaps the greatest piece of luck in the whole story is that the penicillin isolated in the laboratory in 1940 and early 1941 was massively impure. Only 1% to 3% of the material injected into animals and the first human patients was actually penicillin – the rest was impurity. If any of this had been toxic to animals or humans, then penicillin could not have become the 'wonder drug' that it did.

Norman Heatley ended his lecture by suggesting that the team's greatest luck was that The British Committee on the Safety of Medicines did not exist in 1941. If it had, it would probably have demanded that penicillin be tested on guinea pigs. Guinea pigs are often allergic to penicillin and this could possibly have resulted in the Committee rejecting penicillin on safety grounds.

Another aspect of 'luck' in the penicillin story could be regarded as the financial consequences of the discovery. We have already heard that the Americans, notably Andrew Moyer, patented some of the processes in the manufacture of the antibiotic and that the Oxford team, with the backing of the University lawyers and The Medical Research Council, had decided *not* to patent their discoveries. This meant that very little financial benefit came to Florey and his team of scientists, to Oxford University or to the British Pharmaceutical industry in general. However, the impact of the introduction of the world's first antibiotic on the reputation of Oxford and British science was huge.

As a consequence, when an obscure bacteriologist in Sardinia discovered a new antibacterial agent in sewage in Cagliari he sent his results to the Medical Research Council (MRC) in London, inviting them to take over his work. The MRC sent the results to Florey who then invited Edward Abraham to take on the project. Together with Guy Newton and some contributions from Norman Heatley, this work eventually resulted in the isolation and purification of the Cephalosporin family of antibiotics, which have been even more successful than the penicillins. Crucially these discoveries were patented and three trusts were set up to use this money to benefit the medical, biological and chemical sciences in Oxford and elsewhere. (These are The Edward Penley Abraham Research Fund, The EPA Cephalosporin Fund and The Newton Abraham Fund.)

Appendix 3: The Story of Cromwell's Head

On September 3rd 1658 a state funeral was held for Oliver Cromwell at Westminster Abbey. Three years later Charles II ordered the dead body of his father's executioner to be exhumed, hung, drawn and quartered. Cromwell's head was then skewered on a spike at Westminster Hall where the trial of Charles I took place. There it remained for a quarter of a century as a grisly reminder to anyone thinking of crossing the monarchy. However, one day during a storm, the pole holding the head snapped and it rolled into a gutter. There it was picked up by a surprised sentry, probably dipped in tar and then Cromwell's head, by now rather battered, passed through various private hands until in 1815 it was sold to Josiah Henry Wilkinson. He had the head examined and its authenticity analysed, before coming to the conclusion that it was, indeed, that of Oliver Cromwell.

Now known generally as the 'Wilkinson head', in part to distinguish it from various other skulls which were occasionally put forward as belonging to the late Lord Protector, the remains passed through several generations of the Wilkinson family. The head was minutely examined several times during the early and mid-twentieth century, subjected to close medical examination, photographed from different angles, X-rayed, weighed and measured, compared with other human remains and with assorted likenesses of Cromwell and discussed in a variety of learned, academic papers. Some of these exercises proved inconclusive and the uncertainty increased public demand for a full scientific examination, such that Wilkinson reluctantly allowed the head to be taken for examination by the eugenicist Karl Pearson and the anthropologist Geoffrey Morant. Their 109-page report concluded that there was a "moral certainty" that the Wilkinson head was that of Oliver Cromwell.

Horace Wilkinson died in 1957, bequeathing the head to his son, who wished to organise a proper burial for the head rather than a public display. He contacted Cromwell's old college, Sidney Sussex in Cambridge, which welcomed the idea. There it was interred on 25 March 1960, in a secret location near the antechapel, preserved in the oak box in which the Wilkinson family had kept the head since 1815. The box was placed in an airtight container and buried, with only a few witnesses present including family and representatives of the college. The secret burial was not announced until October 1962.

APPENDIX 4
BACTERIAL ANTAGONISM:
REDISCOVERY BY DUNN SCHOOL STUDENT

This photograph (overleaf) appears on p.243 of Heatley's lab notebook, dated September 24th 1940.

It shows a rare phenomenon which Norman had entitled, 'Example of bacterial antagonism'. His commentary reads:

> *Students in the bacteriology class had been plating out pus. Miss Mercer's plate had the appearance shown below. The pus contained organisms which gave two types of colonies, viz:*
>
> > *1. A small white or cream-coloured, smooth, glistening colony, which proved to be of Gram-positive cocci.*
> > *2. A slightly larger grey, translucent, round glistening colony composed of Gram-negative rods.*
>
> *The plating had been done in the usual way and the whole surface had been covered. It seems that half-way round the plate a patch of some contaminating organism was encountered which was spread over the rest of the plate and inhibited both the pus organisms.*

On the next page of the notebook Norman had written, "It was decided not to investigate further."

This sounds like a lost opportunity. The plate reminds us of Fleming's original *'Penicillium'* plate. However, if Norman's interpretation is correct it could have been even more remarkable because the postulated inhibiting organism inhibited Gram-negative rods (which penicillin rarely does).

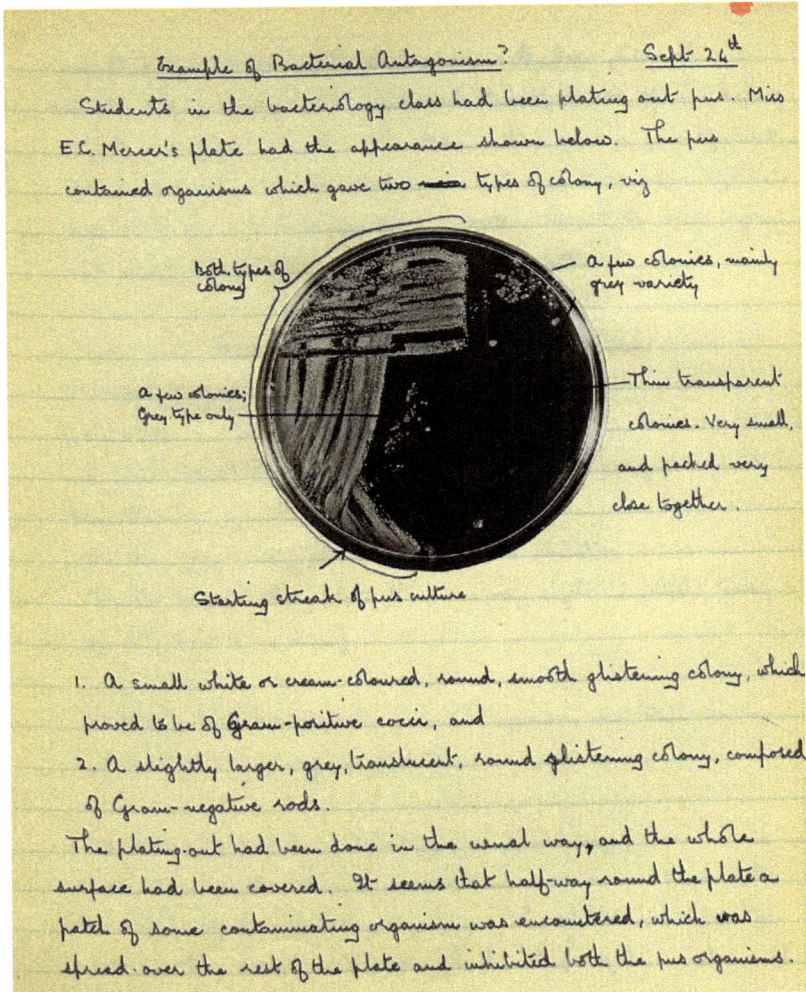

Example of Bacterial Antagonism?   Sept 24th

Students in the bacteriology class had been plating out pus. Miss E.C. Mercer's plate had the appearance shown below. The pus contained organisms which gave two types of colony, viz

Both types of colony

a few colonies, mainly grey variety

a few colonies; grey type only

Thin transparent colonies. Very small, and packed very close together.

Starting streak of pus culture

1. A small white or cream-coloured, round, smooth glistening colony, which proved to be of Gram-positive cocci, and
2. A slightly larger, grey, translucent, round glistening colony, composed of Gram-negative rods.

The plating-out had been done in the usual way, and the whole surface had been covered. It seems that half-way round the plate a patch of some contaminating organism was encountered, which was spread over the rest of the plate and inhibited both the pus organisms.

FURTHER READING

1st Oxford penicillin paper:
"Penicillin as a chemotherapeutic agent." Chain et al.,
   Lancet, 24 Aug 1940, p226.

2nd Oxford penicillin paper:
"Further observations on penicillin." Abraham et al., *Lancet*,
   16 Aug 1941, p177.

Penicillin and Luck, by Norman Heatley (RCJT Books, 2004)

Howard Florey: The Making of a Great Scientist, by Gwyn
   Macfarlane (Oxford University Press, 1979)

Howard Florey: Penicillin and After, by Trevor Williams (Oxford
   University Press, 1984)

The Mould in Dr Florey's Coat, by Eric Lax (Little Brown, 2004)

*Pioneering Physician. The Life of Charles Fletcher, 1911-1995. His
   story as told to Max Blythe* (Words by Design, 2016).